5-MINUTE FOCUS

5-MINUTE
FOCUS

Exercises to
Reduce Distraction,
Improve Concentration, and
Increase Performance

DR. TIFFANY SHELTON MARIOLLE

ROCKRIDGE
PRESS

Interior and Cover Designer: Jay Dea
Art Manager: Hillary Frileck
Editor: Lia Ottaviano
Production Editor: Ashley Polikoff
Author photo courtesy of ©Virginia Conessa

ISBN: Print 978-1-64152-711-8 | eBook 978-1-64152-712-5
R0

I dedicate this book to my loving
husband, Jean Victor, and my
baby girl, Layla. You two will always
be my ultimate focus.

CONTENTS

INTRODUCTION

Imagine being completely focused on a task. You're immersed in it and engaging with purpose and clarity, totally locked in. You've reached that flow that can often feel so elusive, and the task is being completed with understanding and ease. Then suddenly the *cutest* squirrel passes your window and snatches your attention like a thief in the night. Your concentration shatters at the sight of its bushy tail and before you can return to your work, you have to settle in again to find your focus. But then another squirrel runs by, then you get a text, and then you get an email notification. By the time you return to what you were working on, half an hour has gone by and you're not entirely sure how. The flow state has been interrupted and feels very far away. How is it possible that you were working so attentively earlier? Where has your focus gone?

If this sounds familiar to you, you're not alone. More and more people are suffering from what I like to call "*a case of the squirrels*." Even the most well-intentioned high achievers are prone to this kind of loss of focus. It occurs when we set out to do one thing but distractions shift our focus and break our concentration—and it's getting worse. Our society has shaped us to have shorter attention spans than our ancestors. The modern world is full of all kinds of squirrels that run past our metaphorical windows. With social media, push notifications, that nagging pressure to respond to emails as soon we get them, unproductive thoughts and emotions, fast-paced work environments, never-ending text messages, confidence in our ability to multitask competently, and the ever-increasing desire for instant gratification, it's a wonder we're able to focus at all!

Learning to focus may be the single most important skill you can learn to help you live a meaningful life. Yes, improving your focus will help boost your performance and productivity, but it will also help you better align the life you're currently living with your true purpose. Distraction can feel like you're under an evil mind-control spell, one that won't allow you to be the high performer you truly are. Distraction will pull you in a thousand directions; all the while, life just passes you by. You may even find yourself asking one day, "What happened to my life? Why haven't I achieved anything that's important to me?" If you fail to focus on what you value, you will live a life without passion, creativity, and connection to who and what is important to you.

What we focus on we get more of, so it's time to focus on what matters to you. Take control of your focus and take control of your life. After all, we all deserve to feel in control of our minds and our lives.

As a psychologist, neuropsychology assessor, and yoga and meditation teacher, I have helped many people, including myself, learn to improve their focus so they can achieve their goals and live more meaningful lives. My method incorporates neuroscience and mindfulness-based techniques to help people train their brains to concentrate better. I draw upon tools from neuropsychology, third-wave psychology, and Eastern philosophies such as yoga and meditation.

And now it is my goal to help you! Focus is a muscle, and I want to offer you exercises to help you strengthen yours. These exercises are quick, easy to implement, and based in science. They can easily be built into your everyday life and they will help you boost your performance immediately. Mindfulness-based exercises will help you use the power of connecting to the present moment to refocus your brain, while neuroscience exercises offer evidence-based strategies to wire your brain to focus better.

This book will also offer you exercises to improve your concentration skills in a variety of situations, including attending boring meetings, sitting in traffic, and procrastinating. It also includes exercises that will help you focus while experiencing difficult emotions like anxiety. The result of all these focus workouts will help you go from scattered, frazzled, and distracted to focused, efficient, and disciplined.

These exercises are specifically designed to help increase efficiency, productivity, inner strength, and control in your life. This book is an invitation for you to commit to improving your focus and, as a result, your life. With these tools, you can strengthen your focus so that even the most distracting squirrel (think bicycling squirrel juggling plates past your window) won't derail you!

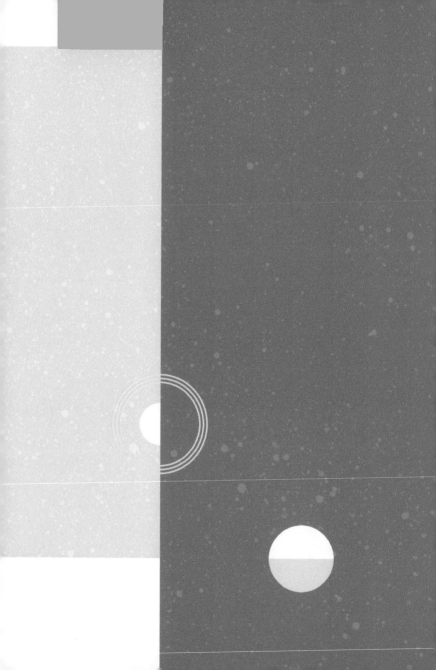

1. Knowing What You Want in Life

You can't bring more focus into your life before deciding what is it that you want. A focused life is one that is directed toward a specific desire. This exercise will help you go from scattered and aimless to purpose-driven and intentional.

Start in a comfortable seated position, either in a chair or on the floor. Close your eyes and take three deep inhales and exhales. Try to release control over your breath and just focus on how you're breathing. Intentionally take a few moments to monitor your inhales and exhales, noticing them without controlling them.

Visualize your happiest self 10 years from now. Imagine how you want to feel, physically, emotionally, and spiritually. In this visualization, take note of how you feel about yourself and what you are most proud of. Take note too of your career, remembering that this is *your* dream, so your career can be anything you want it to be. Think about what you do for a living and how it contributes to your happiness.

Next, take note of the people in your life. Who surrounds you that makes you smile? Who do you vacation with? Even if they don't exist in your life yet, imagine the people who lift you up and surround you on a beautiful day.

Lastly, imagine the most peaceful day. Maybe it's a day off or maybe the day consists of both work and other activities. Visualize this lovely, peaceful day. Once you can see the day in your mind's eye, end by noticing how you feel and what emotions are present during your visualization.

After you have completed the visualization, reflect on what personal and career goals arose during the exercise.

2. The Alert Driver

This exercise will help you become a more alert and conscious driver. Use it to set you up for a mindful driving experience.

Start by taking a minute to address the items on this checklist:

- **Eliminate distractions**. Remove items rolling around on the floor or in your back seat. Turn off the radio. Put your phone on silent or in drive mode.

- **Check in with your biology.** It's best to be hydrated, well-rested, and to have eaten nutritious foods before engaging in this exercise (and in general!). This will set you up for optimum alertness.

- **Take a sniff of your favorite energizing essential oil.** I recommend trying a citrus scent such as lemon or orange.

- **Finish grooming before taking off.** Don't leave tasks such as buttoning your shirt or putting on mascara until driving time.

- **Buckle up.** Safety is the main priority, so be sure to buckle your seat belt before taking off.

Intention. Spend the next minute setting an intention for your drive, before starting the car. I recommend saying the following to yourself: "I intend to be an alert and safe driver."

Mindful driving. For the first three minutes of your drive, practice mindful driving by focusing on what your senses are taking in. This includes the obvious senses, like seeing or hearing, but it also extends to how the car feels while driving.

The point of this exercise is to stay in the present moment as you drive, staying alert and conscious of each moment. If you notice your thoughts drifting or if you begin to think about anything other than driving, gently return your attention back to the present moment. Refocus on your driving experience without judging yourself for drifting off.

3. Replace That Morning Coffee

Neuroscience has revealed the benefits of physical exercise, such as boosting endorphins and energy. Increased exercise wires our brains to focus better throughout the day.

This energizing morning exercise sequence can be done on the floor and will improve your ability to focus throughout the day.

1. Alternating elbow-to-knee crunch: Start lying on your back, knees bent, and hands clasped behind your head. Keeping your chin to your chest and elbows wide, lift up and twist gently so that your right elbow touches your left knee. Then lower back down. Alternate sides, and repeat for 25 crunches on each side.

2. Plank: Begin on your hands and knees, with your hands aligned directly under your shoulders. Slowly lift your knees, creating a straight line with your body. For support, push your hands into the ground as you squeeze in your abs. Hold for 30 seconds.

3. Right-arm side plank: Shift your weight to your right side and slowly shift your body to face to your left. Raise your left arm to the sky as you balance on the right hand and right side of your foot, stacking the left foot on top of the right. Hold for 30 seconds.

4. Plank: Lower the left arm down and pivot to plank position.

5. Push-up: Immediately complete one push-up. To avoid injury, be sure your hands are directly under your shoulder. Engage your core to protect your lower back.

6. Left arm side plank: At the top of the push-up, pivot for a side plank, balancing on your left side.

7. Plank to Child's Pose: Return to plank position and gently lower your knees down. Push your hips back, lowering your bottom to your heels, while lowering your head to the floor. Rest in Child's Pose for 30 seconds.

4. Make Meditation Easier

This exercise will make it easier to focus before meditation, increasing clarity and concentration. I call this exercise the PIC, for posture, intention, and controlled breathing.

P—Take two minutes to establish the correct *posture* for meditation. Start by sitting in a comfortable cross-legged seated position on a meditation cushion or blanket. For increased support, elevate your hips with another cushion or rolled-up blanket to support your knees. Then gently press your hands into the ground, while lifting your tailbone off this second cushion. Tuck your tailbone, lengthening the spine down toward the ground, and gently lower down. Further support the spine by bringing in your lower rib cage and rolling your shoulders up and back. Place your hands on your knees with palms facing up. Lower your chin to your chest and lift the crown of your head to the sky. Release any tension in your eyes or jaw.

I—Take a minute to set an *intention* for your meditation practice. What is your motivation for meditating today? Mentally state your intention to yourself. For example, you might say, "My intention is to stay in the present moment as I meditate today."

C—Finish this exercise by taking two minutes to engage in *controlled breathing*. Take three deep, cleansing breaths to begin. Then, breathing through your nose, begin to count your breaths until reaching 10, and then restart counting. Each cycle of inhales and exhales counts as one. Starting over at 10 will help build your concentration and prepare you for meditation. If you go over 10, gently notice this without judgment and start back over at one.

5. Case of the Mondays

Get rid of those Monday blues and start your week off with clarity and ease. Use this exercise to increase focus and go into your week with confidence. After habitual use, you will no longer dread Mondays and actually start to like them!

First, take a moment to reflect on your top two goals for this year and why you want to achieve them. What is it you want to accomplish this year? What's motivating you to achieve these goals? Why do you believe it will happen?

Think about what is motivating you and take stock of your own personal confidence in achieving them.

Then, with your goals in mind, take a minute to set your priorities for the week as they relate to your yearlong goals. These priorities should directly align with your goals and move you closer to what you want to achieve this year.

Lastly, spend the remaining three minutes using block scheduling to break your weekly goals into tasks during the week. You want your list of tasks to be short and realistic. Only spend a maximum of three minutes doing this; the abbreviated time frame will ensure that your list of tasks remains condensed. Block off time each day to work on tasks that benefit your priorities. Be sure to be realistic when blocking off time by giving yourself more time than you think you will need for each task.

To avoid burnout, be sure to also block off time to rest and have fun.

6. Start Each Workday Off Right!

In Exercise 5, you identified realistic goals and planned out what you'd like to accomplish during the week. This exercise is an extension of that and will help ensure that you're already focused and alert when sitting down to your work.

Before starting work each day, take one minute to review your daily calendar and make a realistic to-do list based on what tasks and appointments are scheduled.

Spend the next minute reflecting on your intention for the day. A focused day starts with an intention that guides its direction. Decide on your intention for the day and say it in your mind. Your intention can be for happiness, productivity, or even calmness. Whatever it is, be sure it is clearly stated before you start your day.

Lastly, spend three minutes visualizing how you want your day to go. Imagine your ideal day from start to finish. See yourself getting your work done and imagine the pride that will come from accomplishing each task. See yourself avoiding distractions and managing anything that might throw you off. Visualize yourself taking breaks and finding joy in the day. Make this visualization as real as possible by taking note of the emotions that accompany each part of your day. When the three minutes are up, end the visualization and set forth to accomplish your best day yet!

7. Focus Even During the Most Dreaded Task

There are some tasks that we resist doing with all our being. This preparatory exercise will set you up to complete even the most dreaded of tasks, using motivation, prioritization, and pleasure. Use this exercise to decrease procrastination and get that dreaded task done.

Motivation. Start by taking a minute to recall why you want to get this task done in the first place. Tap into your motivation for getting it done.

Prioritization. Take a minute to adjust your calendar to prioritize your dreaded task. Make this task the first thing you do that day. As soon as you sit down to work, start with this dreaded task so your brain has something to look forward to later in the day. This will also reduce anxiety from having to think about doing it all day.

Pleasure. Take the last three minutes of this exercise to set yourself up for as much pleasure as possible while completing this task. Turn on some relaxing (lyric-free) music, grab your favorite snack, and make sure you are dressed as comfortably as possible. Another great way to increase pleasure while you are working is to make your environment visually appealing. Add pictures of loved ones to your work space, or a bouquet of flowers to induce feelings of joy as you work. You can also add elements of aromatherapy to increase pleasure as you work, such as setting up an essential oil diffuser using invigorating scents like lemon or orange. If you have pets, make sure the essential oils you choose won't be harmful to them. Some oils can be dangerous to certain animals.

This exercise uses brain science on how dopamine increases our ability to concentrate. Each element of this exercise (motivation, prioritization, and pleasure) is designed to increase dopamine in our brains, which helps us focus better and take action.

8. Rejuvenating Five-Minute Break

The Pomodoro technique, developed by Francesco Cirillo, uses a five-minute break to increase focus while you are working. The five-minute break is a crucial element to the method, allowing your brain to rest and refocus.

Here's how to implement the Pomodoro technique for increased focus and productivity:

- Use Exercise 7 to establish motivation, work priorities, and pleasure for your work session.

- Set a timer for 25 minutes.

- Begin working, committing to staying focused on work until the 25-minute timer buzzes.

- When the timer goes off, stop working and make a note that this is your first break.

- Set your timer for five minutes and engage in something relaxing and non-work related. Here are some ideas for your five-minute break:

  One minute of alternate-nostril breathing (nadi shodhana). Start by covering your right nostril with your right thumb. Exhale slowly and fully through your left nostril, and then inhale through your left nostril, slowly and fully. Then cover your left nostril with your right pinkie finger while releasing your right thumb from your right nostril. Exhale and inhale through your right nostril, cover with your right thumb, and repeat the process on the left side. Continue for one minute.

Shoulder and neck stretches. Sit on your right hand and tilt your head to the right and slightly forward. Hold for 15 seconds. Repeat on the opposite side.

Seated Figure Four. Start by sitting in a chair. Flex your right foot and bring your outside right ankle to sit on your left knee. Lift your arms to the sky and slowly bend forward over your lap. Hold for 30 seconds and repeat on the opposite side.

Cat/Cow back stretch. Sitting on the edge of your chair, place your hands on your knees. Slowly lower your chin down, scoop your belly inward, and tuck your tailbone (cow). Hold for five seconds. Slowly lift your chin up toward the sky, stick out your chest, and arch your back (cat). Hold for five seconds. Continue cat/cow sequence for one minute.

- Next, repeat the cycle of working 25 minutes, then taking a five-minute break. When you have reached four five-minute breaks, your fifth break can last longer, anywhere from 10 to 20 minutes. Then, reset your count, and start the technique from the beginning.

This technique trains your brain to focus in short intervals and improves concentration over time.

9. The Devil Is in the Details

Detail-oriented work often drains our ability to concentrate. This candle meditation (*trataka*) will help increase your concentration skills and strengthen your focus muscle.

This exercise will require a candle. Start by sitting in a comfortable seated position, either cross-legged on the floor or in a chair. Light your candle and place it about three feet in front of you. Place your hands on your knees, palms facing up. Gently gaze at your candle's flame.

Using mindfulness, consciously observe the flicker of the fire, its movement, its smoke, and its colors. Concentrate solely on the fire's existence, without judgment. If you notice thoughts arising that take you away from observing the fire, gently and nonjudgmentally shift your attention back to the fire.

Start with two minutes for this meditation and gradually work your way up to five minutes, adding 30 seconds each time you practice. This practice will strengthen your ability to concentrate on details, strengthen eye muscles, improve your ability to make decisions, and reduce anxiety.

10. Reading Boring Material

Having to read boring material can feel like a death sentence. This five-minute reading exercise will help you improve your ability to focus while reading boring material.

To build this skill, start with committing to five minutes of reading something boring each day. As you are reading, use the following skills to increase your ability to focus:

1. Before you begin reading, take a moment to make sure your environment is distraction-free.

2. Start by taking three deep breaths to bring yourself into the present moment.

3. Eliminate visual distractions by using a bookmark or piece of paper to cover the lines below the line you are reading. This will help you focus on one line at a time.

4. Highlight or underline important information and take notes summarizing what you've read. This will help you encode important information, to emphasize points in your mind.

5. Reread complex sentences. Repetition will allow your mind to better understand what you are reading, and hence increase focus.

6. Try to add elements of pleasure to your reading experience. Listen to relaxing music or enjoy your favorite hot beverage.

7. If you notice you are distracted by thoughts, take a moment to take three more deep breaths before refocusing on the reading task.

Start small and build on this skill, with small bursts of reading each day. By committing five minutes a day to this exercise, reading dry material will no longer feel like a punishment, and you'll gain the power to focus and retain valuable information.

11. Become a Bookworm

Do you find yourself wanting to read more, but find it difficult to become the bookworm you wish to be? Sometimes it can be difficult to focus, even when we are reading material we truly want to consume. This short exercise will help you finally get to those pleasurable books you've been dying to sit down and read.

Start by making a list of the books you want to read. Next put a number beside each book, representing the order in which you intend to read them. Then schedule a weekly time in your calendar that you will dedicate to reading. This must be a time that is nonnegotiable and that you can dedicate solely to reading each week.

Next, take a moment to preplan where you will read. Having a dedicated reading space will support your reading practice.

Finally, pick a person in your life you respect and let them know which book you are reading (or intend to read). Tell them that you would love to talk with them about the book when you finish it. Making yourself accountable to someone else and planning ahead will increase the likelihood of following through.

12. Writer's Block

Most people are required to write in some form in their daily work, whether it's emails, pitches, strategic plans, grants, etc. But writer's block—a nasty combination of procrastination, inattention, and dread—can be a difficult distraction to overcome. This brief strategy will assist you in cutting through writer's block and getting down to business.

Begin by setting an intention for your writing session. Ask yourself why you want or need to complete your writing task, and what you hope to achieve. Then, take three minutes to complete a quick and simple outline. Don't worry about having all the details at this point—the idea here is to do this quickly, without thinking much about it or judging what you write.

Next, develop an "ugly first draft." Writing coach Ann Handley developed the ugly first draft philosophy. The idea is to take the pressure off your first draft by encouraging judgment-free writing. Self-editing is not allowed in the ugly first draft stage, so allow yourself to make mistakes. The final step of this exercise is to establish and then repeat a mantra you can use to remind yourself that this first draft doesn't have to be perfect.

Example mantras:

- "This first draft doesn't have to be perfect, it just has to get done."

- "I'm just going to get this down on paper, and then I'll make it magic."

- "Don't think, just write!"

Do this quick exercise when you face writer's block to help you home in on your intention and ideas, and push through dread. This will help you focus on what you want to write and leave writer's block in the wind.

13. Create Focused Content

Many high performers and go-getters are tasked with some form of social media responsibility, either for their personal brand or their company. With all the other demands that come with being a go-getter, sometimes it can be difficult to create a focused and effective content strategy. This exercise will help you streamline your strategy, so your social media endeavors will have the greatest impact.

First run through this checklist to make sure your content is focused and effective:

- How will this content align with the purpose of my brand?

- What problem am I helping my followers or customers solve?

- How can I integrate my brand's aesthetic into this content?

- How can I ensure that the copy is cohesive with my brand's voice?

- How can I optimize this content so my target follower or customer can find it?

- How can I make this content visually appealing?

- Is there a way to make this content stimulating or entertaining?

- How can I incorporate a call to action (e.g., likes, comments, clicking a link, purchasing a product, etc.)?

This exercise is easy yet powerful. Use this simple checklist to ensure that every piece of content is streamlined and makes an impact. This will ensure that your brand has a focused message that is clear and memorable.

14. Creative Arts

Whether it is due to a lack of inspiration or a distracted mind, there are times when we just can't get the creative juices flowing. This exercise will help you get into a flow state for optimal creativity.

A flow state is a spontaneous occurrence. We can't force it to happen but we can set the scene for it to occur. We will use the last five steps of Ashtanga Yoga to help us induce a flow state.

- **Step 1: Pranayama (breath work)**—Start with a quick breathing technique. Inhale through your nose to the count of four, and exhale to the count of eight. Repeat this for four cycles.

- **Step 2: Pratyahara (withdrawal of consciousness)**—Take a minute to notice any sensations, thoughts, and emotions (e.g., tension, apprehension, dread) that arise, and try to let them go without engaging with them. This taps into the executive control centers in our brains that are needed to focus.

- **Step 3: Dhyrana (concentration)**—Eliminate distractions. Create a quiet, safe space by blocking out any distracting noise. Then, add something pleasurable to your experience (e.g., a piece of chocolate) to increase dopamine, which helps with attention. This step taps into the alerting and orienting systems in our brain, another crucial element for focus.

- **Step 4: *Dhyana* (holistic awareness)**—This exercise uses the right side of our brain to ready all the systems needed for focused creativity. Take a minute to visualize yourself creating. See yourself in the zone, experiencing feelings of joy, inspiration, and freedom.

- **Step 5: *Samadhi* (meditation or flow state)**— When applied to creative work, flow state is equivalent to a meditative state: a state of pure being, releasing attention, concentration, and contemplation. This exercise is designed to set you up to start creating from this space of pure being.

15. Test Anxiety

Life is full of challenges and tests. Even when we have done everything possible to prepare, test anxiety can steal our confidence and make it incredibly hard to focus. This exercise will help you compose yourself before a test or challenge and make it easier to concentrate.

Begin by taking two minutes to reflect on your ability to pass this test. Remind yourself that you prepared and that you have what it takes. Recall times when you passed difficult tests in the past and tell yourself that you are capable of meeting the challenge ahead of you.

Next, take two minutes to slow down your heartbeat. To do so, simply take your left index and middle fingers and place them on your pulse on your neck. For the next two minutes, inhale as deeply as you can (try counting quickly to 20) and exhale using the same pace. These long, deep breaths will send signals to your brain that you are safe, which will help you relax.

End this exercise by taking a moment to boost your confidence. Repeat the following mantras to yourself as you stand in a Superman pose, with your chest out and hands on your hips:

"I am capable."
"I am confident."
"I have what it takes to ace this exam."

16. Nervous Mind, Distracted Mind

When we feel nervous, our thoughts tend to race, making it impossible to concentrate. Whether it's an interview or an important meeting that's making you nervous, use this simple exercise to help you calm down and concentrate on the task at hand.

Find a space where you have privacy and feel safe to close your eyes. Set a timer on your phone for five minutes.

In a comfortable seated position, close your eyes and release any tension in your face, shoulders, lower back, and legs.

Begin to imagine sitting on a pristine beach. Imagine the colors of the beautiful ocean and sandy beaches. Imagine the gentle sun hitting your face, and feel yourself sitting, carefree, on this divine beach.

As you sit on this beach, notice the ebb and flow of the ocean as the waves gently come in to meet your feet, before gently pulling back into the vast ocean. Notice the rhythm of the ocean waves, and begin to match your inhales to waves coming in and your exhales to waves being pulled out to sea.

Continue breathing with the ocean, sitting peacefully on the beach, until your timer goes off.

This mini vacation in your mind will distract you from racing thoughts and calm your nervous system. Once calm, you will have the freedom to concentrate.

17. Savor Every Bite

Food can be one of life's great pleasures—one that we all deserve to enjoy—but with the hustle and bustle of life, many times our meals are taken for granted and laced with distraction. This exercise will help you begin to enjoy meals again, by teaching you to slow down and focus while you eat.

During your next meal, take five minutes to practice mindful eating. Begin by eliminating distractions in your environment, such as your phone or paperwork. Avoid multitasking and devote these five minutes solely to eating.

First, engage your sense of sight, taking note of your food visually. Notice the colors and shapes of your food. Notice how your food sits on your plate. Next, engage your sense of smell. Take a whiff of your food and try to identify various scents and flavors; notice any memories that arise as you think of past meals.

Now begin to slowly eat your food, taking your time and being mindful of each bite. If you are using your hands, take note of how the food feels in your fingers. If you are using utensils, notice the process of getting the food on your spoon or fork. As you chew, notice how the food feels in your mouth. Notice all the sensations that arise. Engage your sense of taste, and truly savor each bite, noticing the flavors and how they make you feel.

Stay mindful of the experience even as you swallow, taking note of the body sensations you experience in your throat and stomach. Continue eating slowly and mindfully in this way for at least five minutes. The more you practice mindful eating, the better you will be at slowing down and savoring your food.

18. Distraction-Free Connection

We have all been to a restaurant and seen that couple that's more engaged with their phones than with each other. We all intend to be available when we connect with loved ones, but sometimes technology can be an addictive distractor. Practice this exercise with a loved one to begin reconnecting at a human level and increase intimacy.

Start by setting an intention to focus on connecting with your loved one without distractions. Set aside five minutes to converse with them. Once you get their buy-in, use the following GEM strategy to connect with your loved one.

Gratitude: As you talk to your loved one, find things about them that you are grateful for. These can be things they have done for you or characteristics they have that you admire. Share with them what you appreciate about them and notice how you feel as you share.

Empathize: As the conversation flows, incorporate empathy to show that you understand and care about what they are saying. This is a verbal way to validate your loved one and show that you care. Try to summarize what they have said and find ways to verbalize that you understand their point of view and agree with what they are saying. Even if you don't entirely agree with their point, find something that you can substantiate from what they are saying.

Mirror: This is a nonverbal way to communicate validation and understanding. Use your body to show that you care. Lean in as the person speaks. Make eye contact as they share. Mirror their facial expressions and tone of voice as authentically as possible.

Each step in this GEM strategy helps build connection and warmth between people. Practice connecting in the present to help shape your ability to connect without distractions.

19. Focused Cooking

This exercise will help you follow even the most complex recipe and stay focused while cooking. This is a five-minute preparatory exercise to set you up to cook with clarity.

The purpose of this exercise is to increase clarity of instructions, wrap your brain around the timing of the recipe, and prepare everything you will need to have at your fingertips. Start by reading the entire recipe without taking any action. Reread any sections that are complex or confusing. Make notes ahead of time that summarize the timing for each component of the recipe. Highlight important considerations that the recipe notes to help you stay alert to these items. Next, spend the next couple of minutes placing all your ingredients on the counter. Finally, take a minute to gather all the utensils you will need to cook.

This is a very simple preparation exercise that will get you in the habit of setting the scene to focus when you cook. It may not seem like rocket science, but just adding this simple strategy to your cooking routine can make all the difference in your ability to follow a complex recipe. By preparing in this way before you cook, you have the freedom to focus on the actual cooking once you begin.

20. Avoid the Afternoon Crash

It's common (and biological) to feel yourself slowing down in the afternoon. This breathing exercise will help you feel revitalized and avoid the afternoon crash, with a rejuvenated and focused brain.

Start by sitting up straight with your shoulders down and back, and the crown of your head toward the sky. Take five cleansing breaths, inhaling slowly through your nose like you're smelling a rose, and exhaling slowly like you're blowing out a candle.

Now, you will begin the skull shining or *Kapalabhati* breathing technique. Place your right hand on your lower belly, just below your belly button. Slowly inhale, sending air to your lower belly. Then, quickly and forcefully, push air out through your nostrils as your lower belly contracts inward 10 times. These exhales will feel somewhat like snorting, and you will feel your lower belly contract quickly in and out as you actively push out air 10 times.

Next, allow a passive inhale through your nose, filling your lower belly once more with air. Then, quickly exhale 10 times as before.

Repeat this cycle until you have passively inhaled and actively exhaled in this way five times. Follow this cycle with five cleansing breaths, slowly inhaling and exhaling. As you breathe deeply, notice any body sensations, such as heat rising in your body. Finally, repeat the five cycles of skull shining breath followed by five cleansing breaths two more times.

This five-minute exercise is simple yet mighty! It is known to energize the body and invigorate the brain by circulating cerebral spinal fluid, discharging carbon dioxide, and heating the body. Also, practicing being fully present by controlling and counting your breaths helps strengthen your brain's ability to focus. Use this tool to combat mental fog after lunch, and say goodbye to the afternoon crash.

21. The Long Road

Long-term focus can be difficult given the many distractions that can pop up over time, including boredom and low motivation. This exercise will help you develop the road map necessary to focus throughout your long-term journey, without letting distractions take you off course.

First, set your intention. What is the purpose of this long-term project? Is it to achieve a personal goal? Is it a work project that is integral to your larger performance? What do you intend to achieve with this project? How will completing this long-term project make an impact in a way that aligns with your values? How do you want to feel when all the work is done?

Next, make a list of all the smaller projects that will need to be done to complete the larger task. This will be your road map and will help you avoid getting distracted or overwhelmed. After you make this list, put the tasks in order of priority and focus on one smaller task at a time.

Your road map will help you connect with the purpose of the project, and the small success of completing tasks will prompt dopamine releases in your brain, increasing your ability to concentrate on

this project long-term. Beyond motivation, break-
ing your project into smaller tasks will make the
long-term project more manageable in your mind
and help you avoid feeling overwhelmed, which is the
ultimate distractor. Creating this road map will help
you wrap your brain around your long-term project,
giving you greater focus on your journey.

22. Memorizing Material

Have you ever sat down to memorize important information but your method for memorizing was so boring that you couldn't stay focused? This exercise will allow you to practice memorizing material in a way that will keep your mind engaged and attentive.

For this exercise, practice memorizing a small amount of information—no more than a couple of paragraphs or an equivalent amount of auditory information. Practice the following strategies in order for one minute each:

- First, use pen and paper to **rewrite** the overall summary of the information you are trying to memorize into one to two sentences. This will help your brain focus on the details while also encoding the most valuable points. Then, take a moment to **color-code** the highlights of the passage, using a yellow highlighter, followed by a red underline of the highlighted information. Studies have shown that using warm colors enhances our ability to focus and hence memorize.

- Using your summary above, try to create an **acronym** of the most important factors. This technique uses verbal cues to help you concentrate.

- Then, in order to add more context to rote information, try to create meaningful **associations** in your mind. For example, whenever I want to help someone remember my name I say, "It's Tiffany, like the jewelry store."

- Create a visual **story** in your mind, using vivid and memorable images to depict the information you need to memorize. This can be particularly helpful when trying to focus on memorizing a sequence of events in order. The mnemonic uses visual cues to increase our ability to retain information.

- Lastly, try to repeat the information you've been memorizing **aloud.** This will highlight whatever information you haven't memorized yet, and cue you to go back and focus on memorizing those details.

Memory starts with attention and focus. After all, we can't remember what we can't pay attention to. Repeating these exercises also helps our brains focus during the latter two components of memory: storage and retrieval.

23. Best Days of Your Life

Sometimes the emotions of a big day can distract us from actually enjoying the moment. How many times have you heard people, maybe even yourself, say, "The day went so fast, it just passed me by." This exercise will help you actually savor those important days in your life and allow you to focus on being present.

This is a three-minute exercise that will help you concentrate on enjoying your most special days. Practice it as many times as you'd like throughout the day, but intentionally set aside some time at the beginning, middle, and end of your day to practice this technique.

Start by taking three deep belly breaths. Next, use your five senses to notice everything around you. What do you see, hear, feel, smell, taste? Notice what emotions you feel and what thoughts are running through your head.

Then, take a few mental snapshots of the moment in your brain. Pretend your mind is a camera and take a moment to memorize this moment and everything you feel about it. You may even want to say the word "click" as you glance around and take your mental photos. End with three additional deep belly breaths.

Whether it's a wedding, graduation, birthday, or any other special day, this exercise can help you savor the day. This is a grounding technique that helps you focus on the day in a memorable way, allowing you to take in the present moment and intentionally savor all its glory.

24. That Big Presentation

It can be devastating to walk away from giving a presentation and feel like you didn't fully convey your message. Whether it's distracting questions, nervousness, or going off on tangents, there are many things that can deter you from a focused message. This exercise will help you stay focused on your message as you present, so that your presentation is impactful and efficient.

Begin by spending three minutes writing down the main ideas you want your audience to take away from the presentation. What are your objectives? How do you want your presentation to impact your audience? What are the concrete examples you're providing to ensure this?

Next, spend two minutes taking deep breaths as you visualize yourself conveying your points with focus and poise. See yourself managing questions in a thoughtful way that circles back to your main points. See yourself breathing and speaking at a normal pace. Visualize yourself feeling proud and confident as you speak. Lastly, imagine your audience members engaged in your talk and walking away with a clear message.

Taking time to clarify your message and envision yourself conveying it efficiently is a powerful strategy to help you communicate in a focused manner. Use this strategy as a final step in your preparation for your big presentation, to increase your ability to deliver a concentrated message.

25. Under Pressure

If we think about what physical pressure does, we realize that it causes an extreme amount of tension and compression. High-pressure mental situations, like deadlines or work evaluations, also cause significant amounts of anxiety and physical tension. These periods of high mental stress are analogous with physical compression, as anxiety causes us to narrow our perspective to our fears. To combat this, try this easy mindfulness strategy to help you focus in high-pressure situations by calming the mind and relaxing the body.

First, sit in a comfortable position and take three deep, grounding breaths. Gently close your eyes and begin intentionally flexing muscles in each section of your body for five seconds, followed by relaxing those same muscles for five seconds.

Start by flexing your feet and then work your way up your body, moving through your calves, thighs, core, chest, back, shoulders, arms and hands. When you reach your head, lower your chin to your chest, gently squeezing the muscles in your neck. To complete this, smile as widely as you can while closing your eyes tightly. With each muscle group, you should be flexing on every inhale and relaxing with each breath you exhale. Be sure not to flex your muscles so tightly that you feel pain. Mindfully notice the difference between your tensed and relaxed states.

Progressive muscle relaxation increases your ability to focus by emphasizing tension and intentionally releasing it. As your mind calms from doing this exercise, your ability to concentrate will improve.

26. Surviving the Most Boring Meeting

We've all been in those boring meetings that should have been replaced by an email. Boring meetings can feel like kryptonite to our focus. The purpose of this exercise is to use engagement as an antidote to boredom. This will tap into the brain's pleasure centers that help us focus.

The next time you're in a boring meeting, try this engagement exercise to reroute your brain to concentrate. When you notice yourself drifting off, spend five minutes actively engaging within the meeting by doing the following:

- **Make eye contact** with the person speaking. Try not to break off eye contact until they have finished making their point.

- **Ask clarifying questions.** Get more concrete understanding on any vague points and ask questions that will make the information more meaningful to you.

- **Take notes.** Even if you feel like you can remember the information, writing notes will help keep you focused on the information being presented.

- Take a couple of invigorating **deep breaths** to keep

your brain alert. Slowly inhale through your nose for as long as you can (try counting to 15 quickly) and exhale for just as long. Repeat once more.

- **Doodle.** If it won't be distracting or disrespectful to other meeting attendees, doodling can help you be more attentive during a boring meeting.

Spending just five minutes stimulating your mind during a meeting is an easy way to quickly wire your brain to focus. Practicing this technique will give you the superpower to survive any boring meeting.

27. Screen Reading

Most people find that reading on a computer screen makes it hard to actually pay attention and comprehend what they are reading. Reading on a computer can be daunting for a variety of reasons, including the instability of the refreshing screen, the screen light, and the lack of tactile aids. This preparation exercise is designed to help you focus better when you read from a computer screen.

Before you sit down to read on your computer, take five minutes to prepare your environment for optimal focus. Start by adjusting the light in the room to minimize any sunlight behind your chair. This will reduce glares that make it difficult to read on a screen. Also adjust the brightness of the screen so it's easier to focus on the words on the screen. Take a moment to optimize the height and angle of the monitor to eliminate distractions such as neck discomfort as you read. Enlarge the font size and adjust the window size of the application you are using to read. You will be able to focus longer if you are not straining your eyes. Increase concentration and comprehension by highlighting and taking notes as you read using PDF reader applications such as Skim, Adobe Reader, or Preview. Finally, end by minimizing distractions in your environment that will make focusing on computer reading easier. See exercise 28 for a detailed exercise to improve overall focus for computer work in general.

These compensatory strategies will help your brain focus while you read on your computer. By taking just five minutes to prepare your environment, you can drastically improve concentration for reading on a computer.

28. Focused Computer Work

There are so many distractions that come with working on your computer, from alerts to emails to falling into Internet rabbit holes. This exercise is designed to keep you focused on the task at hand and to help you concentrate better while working on the computer. The key strategy here is to eliminate distractions before they begin.

Before you begin any computer work, spend three to five minutes doing the following:

- Set an intention for your computer work. Ask yourself what you hope to accomplish and think about how you will know if you are off track from this mission.

- Close all email applications. Set aside another time in your calendar to attend to emails and prioritize your current time for the task at hand.

- Likewise, turn off all social media notifications. Social media has many addictive factors that steal our attention and productivity. Even if you think you will just glance at it for a second, it has the power to suck you in for much longer.

- Put your phone on "Do Not Disturb" mode. Our phones are another thief of our productivity and focus, so it makes sense to eliminate this factor.

- If using the Internet to work, be sure to keep only one to three tabs or windows open at a time. This will eliminate distracting clutter and going off track.

- If you're doing a computer task that does not require the Internet, turn off your Wi-Fi and eliminate the ability to surf the Web altogether.

- Place a sticky note that says *focus* at the top left corner of your computer screen. This will serve as a friendly (nonelectronic) way to remind you to stay on track.

29. Savor Your Time Off

Do you ever find yourself excited to get some downtime, but when it finally comes all you can think about is work? This practice aims to develop your ability to focus on savoring your time off without being consumed by worries about work.

Start by taking a second to connect to the present, breathing deeply and noticing your surroundings. Take in the moment, and intentionally become aware that you are not in your work environment. Notice what makes this place relaxing.

Now bring your attention to your thoughts. When you notice a thought about work, see if you can accept it, versus trying to push it away. Say to yourself, "I am having the thought that ____, and it's okay." See if you can hold the thought lightly, by envisioning it as words bouncing across a screen in your mind.

Next, see if you can tap into some compassion for yourself by saying, "I understand why my mind worries sometimes, AND I can enjoy this moment even if worry is in the background."

Gently release the thought by envisioning your thought written on a piece of paper, then folded up and inserted into a bouncing ball. Visualize that ball being dropped and playfully bouncing away until it's out of sight.

Take a deep breath, and open your awareness to your value of self-care and relaxation. Think about why this is important to you. Then say to yourself, "I commit to relaxing today, even if I have to carry worry with me." Take one last deep breath to close the meditation.

Whether it's your evening off, the weekend, or a long-awaited vacation, you can use this technique to truly focus on relaxing as you take your much-needed break.

30. Cleanup Time

The purpose of this exercise is to help you clean effectively without getting distracted. Many cleaning sessions are wasted because of our inability to focus. This mindfulness practice will help you shape your ability to concentrate on cleaning and make the most of your cleanup time.

First, think about your goal for cleaning. What space do you want to clean, and how deeply do you want to clean during this session? Next, add some pleasure to your cleaning session by playing some music, trying a new cleaning product, or sipping on your favorite beverage. Prepare for distractions by creating a place for things you will clean/organize later.

When you actually start cleaning, treat it as a mindfulness exercise.

How to practice mindful cleaning:

- Tune in to your **breath** as you clean. Try to notice any changes in the rhythm of your breath as you move from task to task.

- Pay attention to **sensations** you feel as you clean. For example, notice things like the warmth of the water as you wash dishes.

- **Watch your hands** as they clean. Become keenly aware of the intricate work your hands perform.

- Pay attention to the **smells** that come along with cleaning. Notice the scent of the fresh laundry, the fragrance of the candles you may light, or even the fresh aroma after vacuuming.

- At the end of the five minutes, take a moment to **appreciate** the work you've done. Be grateful for the clean space you have created in only five minutes. Take a deep breath and thank yourself for your efforts.

This mindful way of cleaning will help you eliminate distractions, focus on your cleaning goals, and help make cleaning pleasurable.

31. Distraction-Heavy Environment

Many of these exercises focus on eliminating distractions to improve concentration. But how do you focus when distractions simply cannot be eliminated, such as when you have to work in a coffee shop or shared office? This meditation practice will teach you concentration skills to help you focus in environments with many distractions.

Take a full minute to breathe in to the count of four, and out to the count of six. Next, spend 30 seconds envisioning yourself concentrating and working efficiently despite many distractions around you. See yourself tuning out the chaos around you and fully focusing on getting your work done.

Next, spend two minutes chanting the following mantra to yourself as you breathe in and out: "I can refocus my mind quickly when I become distracted." The most important part of the practice is this next step, which will help you develop the skills needed to bring your attention back quickly. When you notice your mind wandering away from the mantra, use the Triple R method to bring yourself back:

- **Realize** that your mind has drifted and acknowledge what has distracted you. Was it a thought or a feeling? Or was it something your senses were attracted to, like a sound or something you saw?

- **Release** the urge to judge yourself for getting distracted. Simply release the distraction without getting too attached to it or indulging it any further.

- **Refocus** on your mantra of "I can refocus my mind quickly when I get distracted."

Use the Triple R method as many times as you need to during the two minutes. Remember, the intention is not to be perfect and never get distracted—the goal is to hone your ability to refocus as soon as you get distracted.

32. Do You Hear What I Hear?

This is a strategy that will expand your capacity to focus on what you hear. This is a helpful exercise that uses music to improve your listening skills and auditory abilities. Use this exercise regularly to become more proficient at focused listening over time.

Begin by inhaling slowly through your nose, and exhaling through your mouth as you flutter your lips with enough pressure to make an audible sound.

Now, play a recorded song that has meaning to you or highlights something you value in life. Be sure the song includes vocals and lyrics. Here are tips to practice listening mindfully:

- **Avoid making judgments** about the song. This is not a time to decide if you still like the song or the lyrics.

- Tune in to what you hear and **how each element makes you feel,** emotionally and physically, with particular attention to how the song affects your breathing pattern.

- **Bring your awareness to the sounds** you hear. Notice the tones and vibrations from the instruments. Notice the overall volume of the song, and how it changes throughout. Be curious about the sound of the voice you are hearing, noticing its pitch, volume, and pace.

- As you become fully aware of the pure sound of the music, **become mindful of the lyrics.** Focus on what words are being conveyed and any reactions you have to the lyrics.

- As you notice yourself becoming distracted by things like thoughts, memories, and emotions, gently bring your attention back to the music and **refocus on listening mindfully.**

This exercise essentially trains your brain to focus on what you hear, improving your listening aptitude.

33. Anxious Much?

Let's face it, anxiety is something that many people struggle with, and it definitely impairs our ability to focus. This breathing technique is exceptionally effective at reducing anxiety—check your pulse or heart rate before and after using this technique to see for yourself. For maximum efficacy, be sure to breathe into your belly and make sure that your exhales last longer than your inhales.

Here's how to use deep breathing to reduce anxiety and increase your capability to focus:

1. Start by sitting in a chair with a relaxed body. Make sure you're sitting with both feet on the ground, a straight back, shoulders lowered away from your ears, a relaxed jaw, and calm eyes.

2. Inhale through your nose only, slowly and deeply like you are smelling a rose, to a count of four. As you inhale, be sure that you're breathing all the way into your belly so that your diaphragm above your belly also expands. Diaphragmatic breathing sends a signal to your brain that you're safe, calming the nervous system.

3. Next, exhale just as slowly through your mouth, as if you are blowing out a birthday candle, to a count of six. Exhaling longer than you inhale sends another signal to your brain that you are safe, further calming your nervous system and reducing anxiety. Be sure to contract your belly in as you exhale, releasing all the air.

4. Continue breathing like this for at least five minutes.

Once you complete this exercise, you will see that your anxiety has leveled off to allow you to concentrate better. If you notice that you still have heightened anxiety after completing this exercise, try to distract yourself by counting to 100, and then repeat the breathing exercise.

34. Battle the Blues

Sadness is another emotion that can inhibit our ability to pay attention to anything but our negative thoughts and somber emotions. This exercise helps us shift our focus in the face of sadness, so that we can focus on what we desire. Use this grounding technique when you need to concentrate on something but sadness is getting in the way.

In his book *Hardwiring Happiness,* Dr. Rick Hanson discusses how our brains have evolved to have a negativity bias, whereby they attach to bad experiences and repel good experiences. As such, we need to give our brains extra practice to help them focus on the positive rather than the negative. This grounding exercise will help us do just that.

Tap into the here and now by becoming aware of three things you can be grateful for in this moment.

Next, think about soothing thoughts and experiences. Think about your favorite color. See it vibrantly in your mind.

Now reflect on your favorite food, recalling what the food looks like, how it tastes, and how it smells.

Then focus on one of your favorite people. It can be a character, someone famous, or someone you know. Reflect on what you like about them and what values come to mind.

Now, focus on your favorite time of the year. What do you love about this season?

Next, think of your favorite animal. What makes this animal unique?

Finally, think of your favorite song. How do you feel when you hear this song? Can you imagine hearing it now?

End this grounding exercise by reconnecting with reality. Take a moment to take in your surroundings and notice how you feel.

35. A Remedy for Overwhelm

The remedy for feeling overwhelmed is to focus. Use this reflection practice to refocus your life when you are feeling overwhelmed by its obligations.

Write down the top two goals you would like to achieve in the next 10 years, five years, and year. Don't spend a lot of time here, just jot down the goals that come to you intuitively.

Next, make a list of all the obligations in your life that are making you feel overwhelmed. Be sure to include obligations from all areas of life, including family, work, hobbies, self-care, and financial obligations.

Now, go through your list and eliminate as many obligations as possible that do not align with your priorities. It can be difficult to let go of obligations, but this is a time to be stringent and practice focusing on the things that matter most to you. Once you have eliminated as many obligations as you can, go through the list once more and notate the obligations that need to be completed immediately (within the next few months) with a letter "A," and mark ones that can be put on hold for later with a letter "B."

Using your goals as a guide, go through your list of "A" obligations and order each obligation accordingly. Now when you go to plan your week, you will have a game plan for your priorities, and be clear on where to focus your time.

This exercise helps you come to terms with what you need to focus on, as well as your own limitations. Use this reflection exercise as a strategy to take control of your life in a focused way.

36. Sleep for Focus

According to the National Sleep Foundation, quality sleep plays an important role in our ability to focus, think clearly, and concentrate. This quick mindfulness exercise will set you up to get the quality sleep you need to concentrate the next day.

First, set up your environment for quality sleep by doing the following:

- Make sure the room is as dark as possible.

- Be sure to turn off screens at least an hour before bed.

- Avoid drinking anything other than water for at least two hours before bed.

- Consider quietly playing white noise or nature sounds.

Now, spend five minutes slowly scanning your body. Start by bringing your attention to your toes. Notice the sensations, the weight, and enhance the mindful awareness that you actually have toes. Try to experience the actual feeling of being aware of your toes. Don't just visualize your toes, truly feel the physical sensations. Move your attention up your body, pausing to notice each of the following body parts in the same way: ankles, calves, knees, pelvis and hips, lower abdomen, lower back, upper abdomen, middle back, chest, upper back, shoulders, neck, jaw, nose, eyes, forehead, and crown of your head. Then, reverse your awareness, scanning your body from your head to your toes.

More than likely you will fall asleep peacefully before you finish this scan, setting you up to focus with ease the next day. If you have not fallen asleep, stay completely still and repeat the scan as many times as needed.

37. Banish Burnout

Burnout is like an evil witch that steals your energy and mental clarity. When you realize you are burned out and overworked, it can feel daunting to think about recovering. This is a quick mindfulness meditation that you can do the moment you realize that you are burned out to kick-start your recovery and increase mental clarity.

Start this meditation in a comfortable seated position, either cross-legged on the floor or sitting in a chair. Begin to tune in to the feelings and sensations that let you know that you are burned out. Take a second to monitor the tape playing in your head, and examine your thoughts with curiosity.

Coming to terms with your suffering, say to yourself, "I am going through a difficult experience." After you get in touch with how you feel, gently turn your attention to your breath. Take three deep belly breaths and then gently release control of your breath. Spend about 30 seconds just observing your breath.

Next, focus on offering yourself empathy by placing your hand over your heart and saying to yourself, "I understand that difficulties are a part of life and everyone experiences them." Keeping your hand on your heart, again take three controlled breaths, followed by observing your breath for 30 seconds.

To close this meditation, offer yourself love. Imagine sending loving energy through your hand to your heart and say to yourself, "This too shall pass. I will feel rejuvenated and rested soon." End again with three controlled breaths, and observe how you feel after practicing self-compassion.

This quick and easy meditation will help you focus by giving you a moment of relief and hope. In the face of burnout, focus can only be regained when we have a moment to refuel and take care of ourselves.

38. Focusing in a Foreign Environment

Because we are creatures of habit, trying to focus on accomplishing a task in a new environment can be very difficult. This visualization will help you get into the zone so that you are able to focus even in a new setting.

Whether you are on vacation, in a coffee shop, or unexpectedly working from home, use this visualization to help your brain focus when you are in a new place. First, to help your mind get in the zone, take a minute to create a comfortable environment. You can add comfort to your new work environment by getting dressed in a similar way that you would in your normal work environment. You can also do things like use your favorite coffee mug, play your usual work music (wear headphones if necessary), or set up your favorite work supplies (notepads, pens, folders, sticky notes, etc.).

Once your environment is as comfortable as possible, spend three minutes visualizing yourself working in your normal work environment. See yourself focused and in the zone of productivity. Notice how it feels as you envision yourself concentrating and avoiding distractions. Notice what sensations arise as you see yourself working diligently. What things are you doing? How is your posture? What distractions are you avoiding? Finally, see yourself completing the task, and notice your thoughts and emotions that come along with this accomplishment.

As you shift to begin working in this new environment, call on those feelings that you noticed in your visualization. See if you bring in those emotions, thoughts, and actions into your new environment. This will allow you to focus using the same motivating elements that fuel your focus in your normal workspace.

39. Communicate with Focus

The key to effective communication is staying focused on what you want to assert. This exercise will help you deliver a focused message that communicates your needs accurately.

Decide what exactly you are hoping to achieve with this communication. Once you've narrowed your focus, fill in this DEESC script to develop your focused message.

1. Describe the situation. Be sure to stick to the facts and to not include any judgments or accusations.

   a. Do say, for example, "When you speak loudly on the phone in our shared office. . ."

   b. Don't say, "When you disregard me and yell on the phone . . ."

2. Express how you feel as a result of this situation. Take accountability for how you feel by using "I" statements.

   a. Do say, "I feel distracted and disregarded."

   b. Don't say, "You make me feel insignificant."

3. Empathize. Showing that you understand the other person's point of view will make it easier for them to hear you.

a. Do say, "I understand you need to make important phone calls."

b. Don't say, "I know you don't really think about other people."

4. Specify what you need or want. This is where you will include what you want from the person, decided beforehand. Be specific and straightforward.

a. Do say, "I need for you to speak at a lower volume when you are on the phone."

b. Don't say, "It would be great if you could maybe try to think about speaking more quietly."

5. Consequences. Explain what will happen if the person can or cannot give you what you want.

a. Do say, "If you can do this, it will make it easier for us to work together."

b. Don't say, "You better be more quiet, or else."

Use this script to communicate with focus and assertiveness. This will help you streamline your message and deliver it with clarity, instead of getting pulled off track with judgments, insults, or passive communication. This script does more than just help us communicate in a nonthreatening way; it gives us a tool to prioritize what we want our communication to focus on and make sure that this priority is communicated in a way that can be heard.

40. Staying Focused

This exercise is designed to increase your sustained concentration abilities, using mindfulness to help you slow down and practice the skills needed to pay attention over longer periods of time.

For this exercise, we will calm the mind by starting with a gentle hand massage. For 30 seconds, gently place the back of your left hand in the palm of your right hand and use your right thumb to firmly massage the palm and fingers of your left hand. After 30 seconds, switch hands and repeat.

Next, place your hands in your lap with palms facing up and then tightly squeeze both hands into fists and hold for 30 to 40 seconds. Slowly release your palms and notice the tingling sensation in your hands. Keep your attention focused on this sensation until it dissipates.

Repeat the hand-clenching and practice staying focused on the tingling sensation once more. When the tingling has completely gone away, repeat the gentle hand massage on both hands.

This easy exercise can be a powerful tool to improve your ability to stay focused. By wiring your brain to sustain attention, you will eventually be able to sustain your attention in a variety of situations.

41. Racing Mind

Have so much on your mind that it's difficult to concentrate? Racing thoughts are a common complaint when people sit down to focus. This exercise will help by taking you out of your head and grounding you in the present.

Begin in a comfortable seated position. Calm your mind by taking a few seated stretches: roll your neck both ways, shrug your shoulders up and down, and stretch your arms up and over your head. Then spend the next three to five minutes using your five senses to ground yourself.

1. See—Start by noticing *five* things you can see in the room you are in.

2. Hear—Bring your attention to *four* things you can hear.

3. Touch—Be mindful of *three* things you can feel (e.g., clothing touching your skin, support of the chair, body sensations).

4. Smell—Notice *two* things you can smell.

5. Taste—Bring your attention to your taste buds, and observe *one* thing you can taste.

By grounding yourself in the present moment, you will automatically take your mind away from thoughts consumed with the past or future. Being present in this way will set you up to focus immediately.

42. Pain, Pain, Go Away!

Focusing on anything else when you are experiencing physical pain can feel like an impossible task. This technique aims to help you accept your pain and enables you to move on to focus on other things as well.

Use this three-step exercise to help your brain hold pain lightly and redirect your attention elsewhere:

1. Accept the Pain—This can seem counterintuitive, but it is a vital first step to refocusing your brain. This will allow you to get out of the never-ending cycle of trying to get rid of the pain and allow you to concentrate on other things. Instead of tensing your body to fight the pain, see if you can relax your body as you notice the pain and become aware of the pain that you are trying to accept. Then say to yourself, "Suffering is a part of life, but it will not last forever." Take a deep inhale and exhale, and try to relax your body even more.

2. Pick one of the following mantras and chant it to yourself for about a minute.

    a. "This pain will not consume me."

    b. "I am stronger than this pain."

    c. "I am experiencing pain but it is not all of my experience."

3. Finally, think about committed action. Using tenets of Acceptance and Commitment Therapy, committed action dictates using your values to guide your behavior. First, start by making a commitment or intention to take action. This means making up your mind that despite pain, you will engage in something you value even if you are still in pain. Ask yourself, what do you value about the task you would like to engage with? Then hold true to your commitment to take action toward these values, even if you have to carry your pain with you.

43. Work It Out!

We all want to get the most out of our workouts, and that means eliminating both internal and external distractions. This breathing technique will help you stay focused and present as you work out, so you can avoid injuries and get the results you desire.

Take the first three minutes of your workout to establish *Ujjayi* breathing, a yogic breathing technique used to increase focus and mental clarity for mindful movement. To do so, you must:

1. Sit comfortably, with your eyes closed or with a soft gaze. Begin with your hand in front of your mouth and imagine that you are fogging up a pane of glass. As you exhale, fog up the mirror of your hand. You'll feel the nice warm breath you've created and you'll also feel a constriction coming from the base of your throat, not from your nose. Repeat the fogging breath one more time.

2. Keep a soft restriction in the back of your throat and inhale through your nose. Practice this in two stages. Start by inhaling through the nose, then exhaling through the mouth (recreating the fogging sensation and noise) and halfway through your exhale, close your mouth and finish exhaling through your nose, maintaining the sound and throat restriction.

3. Continue breathing in this way through your nose, maintaining the constriction in your throat on the inhales and exhales so that the sound is even throughout the entire breath.

4. After establishing your *Ujjayi* breath for three minutes, move into your workout while maintaining this breath. Use your inhales and exhales to mindfully move throughout your workout, matching your inhales and exhales to the movement of your exercise.

44. It's Complicated

There are generally two types of attention: simple and complex attention. Simple attention requires us to focus on one thing at a time. However, complex attention requires us to focus on multiple factors at a time and usually involves manipulating these factors in some way. For example, driving is a great example of our use of complex attention, as it requires us to focus on many things at once. Focusing on more complex situations requires skills that can be improved by practicing simple exercises. This exercise is an easy method to expand your complex attention skills.

This is a brain-stimulating exercise that will generally take you about three minutes to practice. Start with the number 100 in your mind and subtract by sevens until you get to the number two. Then starting with the number two, add by sevens until you get to the number 100. Repeat this serial subtraction exercise, but next, subtract by eights and stop when you get to the number four.

Whether you need to focus on listening while writing, sorting information in your mind, or following complex instructions, this exercise will help grow your complex attention skills. This is because this simple exercise will get your brain practiced at focusing on many factors at once. This strategy will also help improve working memory and acts as a mental distraction to reduce anxiety.

45. Building Concentration

The purpose of this technique is to help you build your concentration muscles. This is another exercise that is simple yet mighty and can be practiced anywhere.

Begin in a comfortable seated position in a space with limited distractions. Close your eyes and take a few moments of silence to observe your breath. Once you feel a bit centered, begin the ABC exercise.

Starting with the letter *A*, think of an animal that begins with this letter. Continue thinking of animals that begin with each letter of the alphabet until you reach the letter *Z*. The key in this exercise is to remain focused on the task and catch yourself when you have drifted away in thought. When you realize that you are distracted, take a second to become aware of the distracting thought and then quickly refocus your attention on naming animals. If you come to a letter that you can't think of a word for, don't spend too much time racking your brain. Instead, try for about five seconds and if no word comes to mind, just make up a nonsensical word and move on to the next letter. When you reach the end of the alphabet, take another moment to center yourself by observing your breath. Then, when you feel centered, start the exercise over but this time using city names instead of animals. Again, notice when your mind is distracted and refocus your attention on naming cities. Then, re-center yourself again and complete the exercise by using each letter in the alphabet to name vegetables.

This is an easy and fun technique to help you shape your concentration skills. To enhance this technique, take time to notice themes of thoughts that distract you and observe how it gets easier to refocus your mind over time.

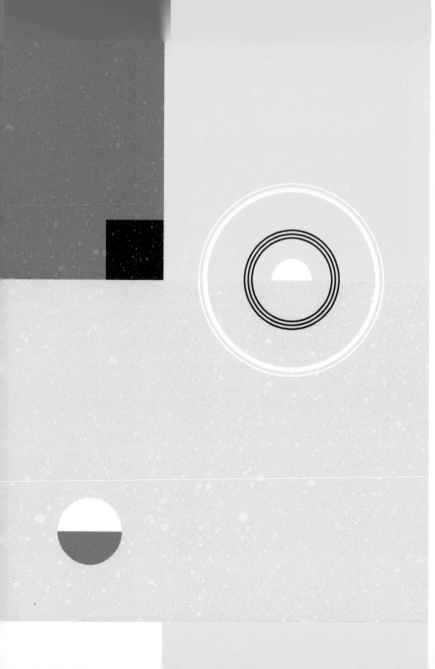

46. Sleepy to Focused

Alertness is a major element of focus. Don't let sleepiness kill your focus. Use this technique to go from sleepy secondary character to the focused hero.

Take five minutes to practice the following and become alert quickly.

1. Sit up straight. Start by getting your body into an alert stance. Take a minute to correct your posture in your chair. This will send signals to your brain that it is time to focus. Plant both feet firmly on the ground. Tuck your tailbone and sit with a straight spine. Roll your shoulders up, back, and down. Place your arms comfortably at your side. Lower your chin and lift the crown of your head to the sky.

2. Drink cold water. Next, drink a glass of ice-cold water. Make sure the water is as cold as you can stand it. The cold temperature will serve as another signal to stimulate the anterior cingulate cortex in your brain for alertness.

3. Laugh. Lastly, take a moment to recall a gut-busting moment in your life. Laughter is a great way to increase alertness. Think of one of the funniest times and allow yourself to laugh out loud.

After this exercise, you will immediately feel more alert and focused. Use this effective strategy any-time you need to combat sleepiness quickly.

47. Your Brain on Nature

Spending time in nature is a great way to improve our focus. Nature has the power to take us out of our head and bring us into the present moment. Being in nature also hones our attention skills.

Start by picking a comfortable spot in nature to practice this exercise. Alternatives to sitting outside (if that is not possible) include looking out a window, focusing on indoor plants, or listening to nature sounds electronically (e.g., tracks of ocean waves, a river stream, or gentle rain). Spend the next five minutes tuning in to the experience of connecting with nature. Here are some things that you may consider as you spend time with nature:

- What do you admire or appreciate about the experience?

- Do you notice any calmness or stillness that you can tune in to?

- Observe your breathing as you experience nature.

- Become aware of any rising emotions.

- Do you notice any natural rhythms or ebbs and flows?

- Is there animal life present that you can appreciate?

After spending some time in nature, take time to reflect on any calmness and mental clarity that arose from the experience. See if you can carry this clarity and focus with you as you continue your day.

48. Focus Now

Procrastination is a famous thief of focus. Many times we have every intention to focus on doing something, but procrastination gets the best of us. Use this exercise to combat procrastination and teach yourself to focus on command.

When we procrastinate we are avoiding the task we want to focus on due to some underlying emotion, such as boredom or doubt in our abilities to complete the task at hand. These emotions can lie under the surface, but we will do everything in our power to avoid feeling them. In this exercise, you will tap into what you are avoiding so you can face it and focus on what you want to accomplish. Ask yourself these questions to get to the bottom of your procrastination.

1. Imagine sitting down to focus on accomplishing your task. What emotions might you feel as you try to focus?

2. What thoughts might run through your head as you complete the task?

3. What are you afraid of experiencing by focusing on this task?

4. How could you cope with these emotions and thoughts? For instance, for boredom, you can brainstorm ways to add more excitement to your task. If you are feeling incompetent, you might brainstorm ways you could feel more confident in completing the task.

5. How might you feel knowing that you pushed through your fears and focused anyway? End by reflecting on how you might feel once the task is completed.

This exercise is a great way to begin facing procrastination and learning how to take control of your ability to focus. Using this technique will allow you to gain a better understanding of the underlying reasons for your lack of focus and enable you to turn it around quickly.

49. Boosting Low Energy

Focus problems may stem from a general lack of energy. Exercise is an effective way to boost endorphins and raise energy levels. Here is a simple yoga sequence to help you pep up and focus better.

1. Start on all fours. Inhale as you drop your head and curve your back to the sky, and exhale as you lift your head and arch your back. Continue breathing this way for one minute.

2. Then, push your hands into the floor, lift your hips, and straighten your legs to come into downward dog position. Hold this position as you breathe deeply for 30 seconds.

3. Next, lift your right heel into the air behind you for 30 seconds, before lowering it down and switching to raise your left leg behind you for 30 seconds.

4. Come back to downward dog position, and lower back down to your hands and knees. Lift your hands off the mat and come up to just your knees. Bring your right knee forward, planting your foot in front of you so that your leg makes a 90-degree angle. Lift your back knee off the ground, coming into a lunge position. Hold for 30 seconds, and repeat on the other side.

5. Come back to hands and knees, and end with one minute of breathing, just as you began.

6. This exercise aims to increase blood circulation to the brain and boost endorphins quickly, for mental clarity and focus.

50. **FOMO**

It can be hard to focus on doing something when we'd rather be doing something else, especially when we feel like we are experiencing FOMO (fear of missing out). For example, say you have to work on the weekend but you know all your friends are enjoying a lovely beach day. This exercise will help you focus even when you are missing out.

Here is how you can prepare your mind to focus when you feel like you are missing out:

- Start by saying no to social media—commit to not checking any social media accounts while you are working. Comparing your day to others will only fuel FOMO.

- Remind yourself of your motivation for working, and take a second to think about how focusing on your work will benefit you in the long run.

- Create a FOMO mantra and write it on a sticky note that you can glance at while you work. For example, your mantra might state, "This isn't my last opportunity to ever have fun."

- Fill your environment with pleasurable things you love. For example, try adding a picture of yourself and a loved one to your work area so you can still feel connection as you work.

- Decide on a special reward for yourself once you finish your work. This will give you something to look forward to and increase your motivation. For example, you may decide to go out for your favorite ice cream upon completion of your task.

This method will help bring perspective to the work you need to get done, and allow you to focus on your own day instead of what others are doing. Kick FOMO to the curb and concentrate on your goals.

51. Attention to Detail

Attention to detail is an important skill that will improve your overall ability to focus. If you struggle with paying attention to visual details, practice this exercise frequently, to further develop this ability.

Choose a quiet space to practice this exercise and take two minutes to embrace stillness. As you sit still, visually take in your surroundings. Notice objects, colors, textures, and shapes. Be aware of any thoughts or feelings that arise. After two minutes of observing in stillness, you can move into the active stage of this exercise.

You will only need a pen and a piece of paper for this next phase. Begin by doodling any abstract figure freehand on the piece of paper. Don't put too much thought into this—just draw. After you have drawn the figure, set your pen aside and take about 15 seconds to meditate on this figure. Study it by paying attention to the details. Once the 15 seconds are complete, turn the page over and close your eyes. Try to visualize the figure you drew. Recall as many details about the figure as you can for 30 seconds and stay mindful of areas of the figure that are difficult to remember. After 30 seconds, open your eyes and study the figure again for 15 seconds. Pay attention to details that were difficult to remember. Then when the 15 seconds are complete, try to recall the figure with your eyes closed. Repeat this sequence one more time to complete the exercise.

Practicing learning in this way will train your brain's frontal lobe to slow down and take in visual details.

52. Overcoming Mental Exhaustion

Have you ever worked so hard that it felt like you were mentally drained upon completion? Brain fatigue is serious enemy of focus. Mindful walking is a great way to reset your brain by increasing oxygen and circulation. Use this exercise to reboot your mind and to focus when you're feeling brain-fatigued.

Begin your five-minute walk by setting an intention to be present with every moment as you walk. Then become aware of your breathing and posture. As you notice your breath, see if you can slow it down. As you notice your posture, try to straighten your spine and lower your shoulders.

Next, begin walking at a slow pace. Begin by noticing your body sensations as you walk. Pay attention to how your foot hits the ground as you walk, and be mindful of each step. Can you tap into any gratitude as you notice one foot after the other working effortlessly in unison?

After about a minute of noticing your body sensations as you walk, begin to mindfully become aware of your surroundings while continuing to breathe slowly and deeply. Without judgment, start to take in what you sense as you walk. Staying in the present moment, consciously observe what you see, hear, smell, feel, and perhaps even taste as you walk. Use the walk as a meditation and try to stay focused on your experience. If thoughts or emotions distract you, be grateful for noticing you were distracted and gently refocus your attention on your mindful walk.

As your walk comes to an end, pay attention to how it feels to stop walking. Take a few deep breaths and see if you can carry any calmness that was cultivated during your walk back with you for the rest of the day.

53. Bouncing Off the Walls

Hyperactivity is a common impediment to being able to focus. If you struggle with sitting still, don't worry—this is a skill that you can build with practice. This exercise helps systematically build your ability to sit still, using gradual exposure.

Unlike sitting while listening to music or a guided meditation, this exercise does not rely on any aids to help you sit still. It truly works on your ability to sit still by improving your internal ways of coping with stillness gradually. This will allow you to combat hyperactivity in any situation. This exercise is best practiced in the morning in a quiet, distraction-free environment. Turn off the TV, put your phone on airplane mode, and eliminate any other distractions as much as possible. This exercise will last five minutes and alternates deep breathing with complete stillness. You can use a timer to stay on track.

1. Start with deep breathing for 30 seconds. Inhale, filling your belly up and expanding your diaphragm as you count to six in your head. Exhale slowly as you count to eight.

2. Then, sit completely still for one minute. Try not to move at all. Notice what sensations, emotions, or thoughts compel you to move. See if you can tolerate any itches or other uncomfortable body sensations. Notice how you are able to tolerate them without being controlled by them. Become aware of any thoughts and emotions that trigger you to move, and tell yourself, "This is just a thought/emotion. I have the power not to be controlled by it." Choose to stay still. This will build your executive control and teach your brain that you have the power not to succumb to every impulse received.

3. After the one minute of stillness, repeat deep breathing for 30 seconds.

4. Then, sit still again for one minute and continue to notice triggers and internal ways of coping with these triggers to move.

5. Repeat deep breathing for 30 seconds.

6. Complete the exercise with two full minutes of stillness.

7. When the two minutes are complete, take a moment to jot down what helped you stay still. Refer to these insights before practicing this exercise the next time.

Eventually, you can work your way up to sitting in stillness for five minutes and add minutes incrementally as you feel comfortable. As you develop your stillness muscle, it will aid in your ability to focus for longer periods of time by improving your executive functioning skills.

54. Focusing Inward

This technique uses the mind-body connection as a tool to improve focus. It is an especially useful exercise to help regulate your mind for focus in times of distress, but it can also be used as a general tool to improve concentration as well.

This technique consists of evaluating our heart rate, engaging in a heartbeat meditation, and a final evaluation of our heart rate. Be sure to sit with a clock or your phone (on airplane mode) with the time in view.

Start by sitting in a comfortable seated position. Place your hands on your knees palms up and then gently wrap your left fingers around your right wrist so that you can feel your pulse with your left index and middle fingers. You can either place your hands resting on your lap or bring both hands up over your chest to rest over your heart. Play with each position before moving on, and use whichever is most comfortable. Then, watching the clock for one minute, count how many heartbeats you can feel. Be sure to concentrate on your heartbeat for the full minute so that you don't miss any beats. Once the minute is complete, try to remember your initial beats per minute.

Then, for the next minute, using your heartbeats as the counter, inhale deeply for six heartbeats, and exhale slowly for eight heartbeats.

Next, release control of your breath and spend the next two minutes concentrating on your pulse. Pay attention to how your pulse feels and imagine your heart pumping blood throughout your body.

Finally, spend the last minute counting your heartbeats one more time. Compare this number to your initial heartbeat count.

You will likely notice that your heart rate has slowed down. This practice of staying with your breath and heartbeat flexes your concentration muscle and your overall capacity for sustained attention.

55. Did You Hear That?

Do you have a hard time focusing on what you hear? If you frequently ask for information to be repeated or find it difficult to pay attention to auditory information, this exercise will certainly help you. This is a simple meditation practice that can build your audible attention skills.

For this exercise, a distraction-free environment is not required. Simply choose a spot where you feel safe enough to close your eyes. Start in a comfortable seated position. Begin to come into the present moment by taking a few audible deep breaths. Inhale through your nose deeply and slowly for as long as you can. Then exhale through your wide-open mouth with your tongue sticking out as far as possible. Make a loud audible "ah" sound as you sigh out your exhale. Repeat this type of breathing for two more full breaths.

Then, begin to breathe normally again and close your eyes. Start to focus your attention on the sounds you hear. You might become aware of sounds that have been in the room that you weren't aware of. Notice the tones and vibrations that come along with these sounds. Notice the volume and length. Become aware of how sounds overlap and which ones pull more for your attention. As sounds arise within your awareness, stay with them for as long as they are present and release them when they have gone. Try to concentrate on the pure experience of each sound, without placing attributions to what you are hearing.

Listen mindfully in this way for five minutes. When distracted, gently refocus on the sounds you hear. This ability to constantly bring our attention back is what builds concentration and focus.

56. Creative Focus

This is a great exercise to try right before you need to focus on a creative project. The technique gets the imaginative juices flowing by stimulating the right brain to tap into creativity. This will wire your brain to focus on creating and set you up for creative success.

For this exercise you will need a piece of paper and either colored pencils or crayons. Start by taking a black pencil or crayon and absentmindedly doodling a large abstract figure on the page without picking up your pen. Make sure the figure has overlapping lines that create different segments within your doodle.

Then, without putting much thought into what you will color, take time to color in each segment with different colors. You can create patterns or use a rainbow of colors. The important thing is to color mindfully, staying present with each stroke. Observe how each color makes you feel. Notice your breathing as you color. Take note of the colors you use and how you choose to place them.

If you find yourself judging your work, remind yourself that the purpose of this exercise is freedom, not perfection. In order to get your mind focused in a creative mind-set, we want to quiet the analytical left brain and stimulate the creative right brain. Spend about five minutes coloring in this way, noticing and being present in the moment.

After completing this simple exercise, your brain should be focused on freethinking, creativity, and staying in the present moment. This is the optimal mind-set to help you focus on your creative project.

57. Focus on the Positive

If your thoughts are focused more on the negative than the positive, you will be at greater risk of depression, anxiety, and many other mental health disorders. Shifting our focus to more positive thoughts requires rerouting neural pathways that have been fortified by evolution and repetition. This exercise is a structured way to access the intentionality and practice required to rewire your brain to focus on the positive.

Practice this quick gratitude reflection nightly, to increase your ability to focus on the positive:

1. Think of three things you are grateful for today. Try to make these three things unique to the day and not repeat something you named the night before.

2. Think about a challenge you're facing in life. Is there anything from this experience you're grateful for? Perhaps there is a lesson learned, an opportunity for personal growth, or maybe an opportunity to help someone.

3. Is there anyone you encountered throughout the day you would like to appreciate? Did anyone give you a compliment, inspire you, or help you? You can take this a step forward and write them a thank-you note.

4. What was your victory for the day? What did you accomplish today that you are proud of? This could be something as simple as making it through the work-day or even appreciating your ability to stay disci-plined with a task. Take a moment to pat yourself on the back for something you did today.

This easy nightly gratitude ritual is a powerful way to help our brains make new connections and expand our perspective beyond simply focusing on negative thoughts. In fact, much research on gratitude has shown how it successfully reduces mental health disorders such as depression.

58. Improve Visual Focus

As you get to know your personal strengths and weaknesses with focus, you may notice that you have more trouble focusing on visual information than auditory information. This is a skill that can be shaped with practice, like any other. This is a straightforward activity to sharpen your visual focus.

First, grab any book or magazine. Open the book to any page full of text and select the longest paragraph. Try counting all the words in that paragraph. This will require attention, concentration, and tenacity. Do not use your fingers to aid you in scanning the lines. Also be sure to count the words in your head, without the use of any guides. Try to foster all your mental strength to concentrate on counting the words until you reach the end of the paragraph.

Try this exercise a few times, before working your way up to counting words on an entire page. Training in this way helps your brain and eyes coordinate improved visual focus. It teaches you the internal skills required to slow down and encode visual information, which will help in your overall ability to focus on this type of information.

59. Single-Tasking

Efficient multitasking is a myth that our current society seems to take as reality. In fact, neuropsychology tells us that there is no such thing as multitasking because our brains are simply not designed for it. In reality, trying to do multiple things at once is a rampant bad habit in the modern world, which ultimately results in poorer-quality work, wasted time, and increased anxiety. Improving our ability to focus on one thing at a time is the only cure to our addiction to multitasking.

This exercise is simple but requires mental fortitude. Don't worry if you start practicing this exercise with your mental fortitude tank on low, as this exercise will help fill that up.

Start seated comfortably in a distraction-free environment. It's best to practice this mindfulness technique in the morning, when you are mentally at your strongest. Pick a word that you have a positive connection with, perhaps a word that embodies your intention for the day, such as "happiness" or "peace." Close your eyes and spend three minutes meditating on this word. Envision the word while also gently repeating it in your head. Be mindful of when your mind strays from your chosen word, and practice bringing your focus back to this single task.

Start with just three minutes for this exercise, and gradually work your way up to five minutes over time. The exercise will condition your brain for single-tasking. The more you improve your ability to focus on one thing at a time, the more productive you will truly be.

60. Calm Down and Focus

There are times when anger rears its ugly head and refuses to allow us to focus on anything other than our frustrations. If you've ever felt angry at a time when you needed to focus on a task, this exercise can be beneficial in helping you calm down and concentrate. This exercise allows us to move from our highly distressed primitive brain to our more rational brain.

Follow these steps to help manage your anger and refocus your mind:

1. Find a comfortable seated position either in a chair or on the floor. If you're in a space where it is feasible to close your eyes, do so. If not, have a soft gaze on a single point.

2. Slowly inhale through your nose as you count to four. Pay attention to the feeling of the air filling your belly and expanding your diaphragm.

3. Hold your breath as you count to four for a second time. Try not to take in any air or release any air during this time.

4. Exhale slowly through your nose as you count to four. Again, feel the air as your belly comes inward and your diaphragm retracts.

5. Repeat steps two to four for a total of three to four minutes.

According to the Mayo Clinic, intentional breathing such as this box-breathing exercise can regulate our autonomic nervous system and improve our mood. Using this technique when you experience anger will give you a powerful tool to help calm your brain and enhance concentration.

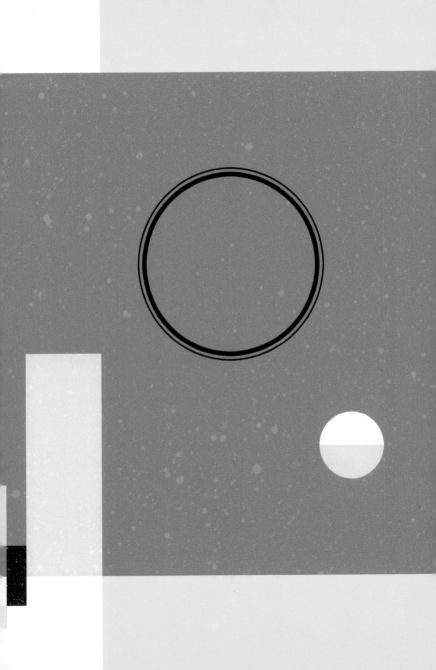

61. Emotional Day

There are times in our lives when we experience a flood of emotions that limit our ability to think clearly. This mindfulness-of-emotions meditation is a great way to regain mental clarity.

Sit with your eyes closed and become aware of your breathing. With an attitude of acceptance, see if you can simply notice your breath, monitoring its ebbs and flows, without trying to control it for one minute.

Once grounded with your breath, shift your attention to your emotional experience. When you get in touch with an emotion, use this script in your head to sit with the emotion mindfully before releasing it and allowing the next emotion to arise. (You can open your eyes to read the script once you notice the emotion.)

- *I am feeling (name the emotion) and I feel it in my (where do you feel this emotion in your body and what bodily sensations occur with it?).*

- *I offer myself compassion and patience as this emotion passes through me.*

- *I do not have to attach to this emotion and will allow it to come in like a gentle wave, and let it go like the tide going back into the ocean.*

- *This emotion will not overcome me; it simply wants to be acknowledged before leaving.*

After you notice the first emotion and run through this script, close your eyes again and allow the next emotion to come to you, and run through the script again. Continue noticing, accepting, and letting go of your emotions for the next four minutes.

By taking the time to acknowledge our emotions, we are starting the process of acceptance. Use this practice to let go and focus on what matters to you in the moment.

62. Flex Your Focus Muscle

Research has shown that exercise has a profound ability to improve focus by increasing oxygen to the brain. This is a great five-minute cardiovascular exercise routine that you can do on your lunch breaks to increase your ability to focus in the afternoon. You can use this exercise routine any time to flex your focus muscle.

Spend one minute doing each of the following:

1. Running in place. It's important that you run at a pace that increases your heart rate.

2. Jumping jacks. Be sure to reach your hands completely overhead and jump out with your legs at least hip-distance apart.

3. Side lunges. Starting from standing, step sideways with your right foot and bend the right knee at a 90-degree angle. At the same time, keep your left foot planted as you extend over to the right and lower your bottom down toward the ground. Be sure not to go lower than your right knee. Come up and repeat this side lunge on the left side. Continue back-and-forth side lunges for a full minute.

4. Squats. Stand with your feet hip-distance apart. Slowly lower down, as if you were going to sit in a chair. Do not go below a 90-degree bend in your knees. Then, slowly rise up. Continue squats for a full minute.

This is a simple way to increase oxygen flow and get your brain focused fast. This exercise routine doesn't require any equipment and is a simple routine to memorize. And although it's simple, it gives your brain the jolt it needs to concentrate better.

63. Decrease Impulsiveness

Impulsivity is a known culprit in impairing our ability to pay attention. Whether it shows up as impatience, restlessness, or poor decision-making, impulsivity has the power to derail our best intentions to focus. If you have noticed that impulsivity has impaired your ability to think clearly at times, this reflection will help you slow down your thinking process.

1. Take note of how impulsivity shows up for you. When are you most impulsive and what does it look like for you? Do you impulsively spend? Does it show up as interrupting people? Does it manifest as impatience when you're trying to pay attention? Does it lead to poor decision-making or reckless behavior?

2. When you find yourself in situations where you exhibit more impulsivity, what intention can you set beforehand? For example, you might develop a mantra for these situations that states, "I intend to cultivate patience and self-awareness as I enter this situation."

3. How can you incorporate pausing in these situations, to allow yourself a moment of calmness and contemplation when you realize the urge to be impulsive? For example, you might consider any of the following mindfulness strategies to take a pause before acting:

a. Deep breathing

b. Relaxing the muscles in your face

c. Lowering your shoulders

d. A quick body scan

Cultivating a sense of calm and patience will aid in your ability to focus in a variety of situations. This reflection will help you increase your self-awareness surrounding your impulsivity and give you a simple plan to improve in this area. Doing so will allow you to stay with the present moment and therefore improve your attention skills.

64. Increase Organization

Disorganization is an easy way to fall into the distraction trap. Organization is a key component of executive functioning that primes our brains to focus. Improving your overall organization skills will certainly aid you in your ability to concentrate, plan, and stay present.

Many people want to be more organized but don't know where to start. Take five minutes to review the following areas and make a list of areas you would like to improve. There are also some helpful tips for each, to get you started.

- **Work and personal spaces.** When organizing physical spaces, give each item a home so everything has a space.

- **Calendars.** When tackling calendars, keep your priorities in mind and be realistic about your time. Use a calendar or planner to block schedule tasks.

- **To-do lists.** Create a running list that you can add to constantly. Then choose priority tasks from this master list to add to your daily to-do list.

- **Big projects.** Break large projects into smaller

tasks. Research project management software and apps and use the ones that work best for you.

- **Thoughts and ideas.** Carry a notebook with you to compile random thoughts and ideas.

- **Notes.** Decide on a universal highlighting and organizational strategy for your notes.

- **Documents.** Create a filing system for your most important documents and get rid of any you no longer need.

Once you have a list, spend five minutes a day working toward organizing each individual area until completion and then move to the next item on your list. Working in five-minute segments will help you build momentum and skill without overwhelming you. It will also help you make organization a habit. Organization helps you focus on what you want when you want, by allowing you to take control of what's in your conscious awareness, rather than letting clutter take the wheel.

65. In Motion

Have you ever tried to focus when you're feeling restless? It's certainly hard to focus when our bodies are fidgeting about. This technique helps you cope with restlessness so you can concentrate on what matters.

First, consider what is contributing to your restless state. Does your fidgeting manifest at certain times or places, or when you feel a certain way? When you have a scenario in mind, take four minutes to engage in the following mindful visualization.

Have a seat in a chair and close your eyes. Bring to mind your scenario, and mentally immerse yourself in it using your five senses. Pay attention to what you see, hear, feel, taste, and smell.

Then bring into your awareness what emotions and thoughts accompany this situation. See yourself calm and composed within it. See yourself breathing slowly.

In this situation, imagine you begin to feel the urge to fidget. See yourself taking a deep breath in and out and resisting the urge. Visualize the energy of the urge as a color in your body, and imagine yourself sending this colorful urge to your brain, to use as fuel to stay present and still. Take a deep breath as you see yourself remaining calm in this scenario.

Now, shift your attention to your current experience. See if you notice urges within yourself to fidget or move about. As you notice these urges, see if you can embody the self you just visualized, by resisting the urge and using that energy to focus on the present moment. Each time you transform an urge to pay attention to the present moment, take a deep breath in and out. Complete this exercise with one final deep breath.

66. All Start, No Finish

We have all had moments when we had the best intentions when starting a task but distractions got in the way and we never finished. There is a special kind of focus required to finish a task that involves awareness, intention, and tenacity. Use this reflection exercise to help you set yourself up for success and get that task done.

- **Awareness.** What are the details of the task that you wish to complete? Write down all the steps needed to complete this task from to start to finish. You will use this list as micro goals to complete one at time until final completion of the larger task.

- **Intention.** Why do you want to complete this project? Why is it important to you and what will you gain from seeing this task through to completion?

- **Grit.** Remind yourself of a time when you pushed through distractions and single-mindedly focused on a task until it was complete. What was helpful in getting you past distractions? What was unhelpful? Then, develop a mantra to remind yourself that you have the capacity to follow through.

For example, your mantra may be, "I believe in my ability to complete tasks that are important to me." Post this mantra in a visible area as you work on your task.

This practical reflection exercise will help you wrap your brain around the key elements needed to focus on a task until completion. It does so by eliminating feelings of overwhelm, increasing motivation, and preparing for distractions.

67. Following Instructions

Following verbal instructions is a unique situation where focus comes in very handy. Often the complexity of multistep directions sends our minds into a tizzy, making it difficult to get a clear picture of what exactly we are supposed to do. Use this exercise to help aid your ability to focus when receiving verbal instructions.

The next time you are trying to understand verbal directions, use this quick strategy to focus better:

1. If the person giving instructions is speaking too fast, don't hesitate to ask them to speak slower.

2. Make eye contact with the person to decrease the likelihood of visual distractions.

3. Try to visualize the process they are describing as they speak.

4. Start by asking clarifying questions to clear up any confusion.

5. Next, repeat back what you think you heard and ask the person to clarify anything you missed.

6. As the person is talking, or as soon as possible, write down what you heard to solidify the information and save it for later.

7. Using your notes, break the directions down into numbered steps.

Overall, using this technique to improve your listening skills will help you focus when receiving instructions. This strategy will also help you follow through with the directions when it is time by increasing clarity.

68. Where Did I Put That?

There's nothing more annoying than feeling like you're constantly misplacing things. This frustration is a direct result of a lack of focus when putting away items. Here is a strategy to help you put away items with a present mind, so that you never have to ask, "Where did I put that?"

Start by thinking of the items you frequently misplace. Then, make a commitment to take a deep breath and become self-aware when you're putting these items away. For example, when you take off your sunglasses, use this as a cue to breathe deeply, pause, and think about what you're doing with intention. Then put the item in its designated home in your house, car, or workspace.

Each item that you frequently misplace should have a home. If it doesn't have one, designate a home for it when you first practice this exercise. Once you initially decide on a home for a specific item, add it to the master list of designated spots for frequently misplaced items. Then the next time you encounter this item to put away, take a mindful moment to breathe, become self-aware, and put the item in its home. Refer to your master list if you can't remember where an item belongs.

With repetition, you will develop habits for returning each of these items to its home over time. Use this strategy to increase your focus when putting items away and end the frustrating experience of constantly misplacing items.

69. Don't Be Tardy

For those who struggle with focus and attention, showing up late can become a major problem. The issue lies with an inability to concentrate when getting ready and time slipping away as a result. This strategy will help you focus while getting ready so you can get to places on time.

Here's a quick checklist you can use to help stay focused while preparing to leave your house.

- Start by focusing on why you want to be on time. What do you value about timeliness and how does it reflect who you want to be?

- Plan to arrive 10 minutes early, not exactly on the dot. This will give you a grace period for any unexpected occurrences.

- Determine, using a map program, how long it will take you to travel to your destination, and use this information to calculate how much time you have to get ready.

- Brainstorm what you realistically have time to do beforehand, given this information, and eliminate any extraneous tasks that you don't have time to get done.

- Set yourself a timer for 10 minutes before you need to leave your house. This will serve as a reminder to start wrapping things up to leave.

- Have access to the time (e.g., on a watch, clock, or your phone), as you get ready.

- Eliminate distractions. You can play some music but eliminate all other media distractions, such as the TV and social media. Also, stick solely to tasks required to get you out the door.

This checklist will help you orient to the present moment and help you manage your time. Use this checklist to focus on what matters as you prepare yourself to leave the house and you prevent distractions from making you tardy for the party.

70. Figure Eight

The ability to focus can be broken down into many different components. Visual focus is an important component of your overall focus abilities. This exercise will help shape your ability to pay attention to visual information.

Practice this exercise in a quiet space with limited distractions. Begin in a comfortable seated position with your eyes closed.

Briefly check in with your body and notice any physical sensations or discomforts. See if you can imagine breathing into this place, creating space and perhaps relief. Spend about a minute checking in with your body and breathing mindfully to areas of discomfort.

Then, open your eyes and imagine a large figure eight on the wall in front of you. Using your eyes only, slowly begin to trace the figure eight you have visualized. Trace so slowly that it takes you a full minute to trace one way, and then slowly trace the figure eight in the opposite direction for one minute.

When finished, close your eyes for a brief break, around 10 seconds. Then, reopen your eyes and trace the figure each way once more.

This exercise will improve your focus skills tremendously. It will build your ability to concentrate on visual stimuli and cultivate the inner discipline needed to concentrate for a fixed amount of time.

71. Learn Something New

Improving focus requires improving your brain. Your brain is like a muscle and learning new things is a great way to exercise it. Learning new information creates novelty, which results in a dopamine burst. This burst of dopamine wires your brain for focus, while the learning also helps form new neural connections in the brain that make it stronger.

Here are some ways to spend five minutes every day learning something new and to wire your brain for focus:

- Learn a new word each day. You can alternate between learning a new word in English and a foreign language.

- Spend five minutes working on a puzzle.

- Practice learning a musical instrument just a little bit each day.

- Read the newspaper or a preferred magazine.

- Search the Internet for research on a subject you are curious about.

- Explore your surroundings. Take a five-minute walk and discover new things in your environment.

- Watch a history channel or a historical movie and see what you can soak up in five minutes.

- Seek out information to learn one new thing in your career field each day.

- Try a new recipe.

These ideas are a great starting point to help you learn something new each day. You may add to this list with other learning activities that you love. The only requirement is to spend five minutes learning each day. Let your curiosity improve your brain.

72. Dopamine Boost

Are you anticipating a day with a particularly high demand for your brain to focus? Dopamine is one of the secret ingredients that wire your brain to focus easily. It is the pleasure neurotransmitter, and our brains have evolved to focus on what brings us pleasure. Besides engaging in passionate and pleasurable activities, there are other ways to plan a day full of dopamine boosts to wire your brain for focus.

Spend five minutes reviewing this checklist and planning a day full of dopamine boosts. Based on research from Healthline dietician and psychology expert Erica Julson and psychiatrist and brain expert Dr. Daniel Amen, here are some helpful ways to boost dopamine naturally:

- Make sure you get plenty of restful sleep the night before.

- Start your day with 20 minutes of cardiovascular exercise.

- Before you begin working, incorporate a 20-minute meditation into your morning. This can be a guided or silent meditation.

- Get plenty of sunlight.

- Incorporate foods like dark chocolate, dairy, fish that is high in omega-3 fatty acids, and probiotics into your diet.

- With your doctor's approval, consider the following supplements: iron, niacin, folate, and vitamin B_6.

- According to brain expert Dr. Daniel Amen, to make dopamine our brain needs tyrosine, which can be found in bananas, avocados, eggs, beans, and chicken.

- Incorporate calming and pleasurable music throughout your day.

Use this checklist to plan a day full of natural dopamine boosts and set yourself up for success on focus-heavy days.

73. How Are You?

Self-awareness is an important attribute of those who have mastered their ability to focus. Having the skills to tap into your emotional state gives you the power to offer yourself what you need to focus. This exercise helps with the first step of becoming aware of what you are feeling.

Use this technique at the start of your day. You will need a notebook or journal and a pen.

Begin journaling about anything you notice regarding your emotional state or how you're feeling in this moment. Write down any thoughts that accompany various emotions, and journal about any bodily sensations that arise as you write down how you feel.

If you are having trouble pinpointing how you feel, reference the following list of common feelings:

Happy	Sad	Disgusted	Angry	Fearful
Stressed	Surprised	Bored	Content	Peaceful
Grateful	Excited	Lonely	Guilty	Ashamed
Disappointed	Frustrated	Irritated	Rejected	Insecure
Startled	Disrespected	Jealous	Nervous	Overwhelmed
Cheeky	Successful	Sensitive	Hopeful	Perplexed
Isolated	Embarrassed	Joyful	Playful	Unfocused

Spend three to five minutes journaling how you feel. Then, use this information to give yourself what you need to focus throughout the day, given your emotional state. For extra help focusing, refer to exercises in this book for that specific emotion. Here is a reference list for exercises to focus on:

- **Boredom**—Exercise 26: Surviving the Most Boring Meeting

- **Sadness**—Exercise 34: Battle the Blues; Exercise 57: Focus on the Positive

- **Anxiety**—Exercise 33: Anxious Much?; Exercise 57: Focus on the Positive

- **Anger**—Exercise 60: Calm Down and Focus

- **Overwhelmed**—Exercise 35: A Remedy for Overwhelm; Exercise 74: Overstimulated

74. Overstimulated

Have you ever found yourself overstimulated by excitement, an overwhelming experience, or many different emotions? This technique will help you soothe your overstimulated brain and reconnect with your rational brain in order to focus.

When you notice that you are overstimulated, take five minutes to self-soothe using the five senses.

- **Sight.** Close your eyes and visualize a soothing environment for one minute. This can be a safe place where you have been before or a fantasy environment that you wish to visit.

- **Hearing.** Repeat a calming affirmation out loud for 30 seconds. For example, you might repeat the phrase, "Peace is my friend and I am becoming calm with each second."

- **Touch.** Spend one minute fidgeting with something in your hands. This can be as simple as a crumpled-up piece of paper, or more specific, like a stress ball or fidget toy.

- **Smell.** Spend one minute indulging in something that smells calming in your environment. Seek out things such as flowers or coffee. If possible, place a few drops of relaxing essential oils (e.g., lavender) on a cotton ball and take a second to sniff the cotton ball mindfully.

- **Taste.** Eat something that can ground you in the present moment, such as a throat lozenge or mint, or mindfully eat something pleasurable like a small chocolate.

Taking five minutes to soothe yourself in this way will allow your brain to calm down and focus. This exercise not only grounds you in the present moment, but it does so in a nurturing and relaxing way.

75. Ruminating Thoughts

Do you ever get stuck on a thought that keeps revisiting you no matter how much you try to push it away? Ruminating thoughts are a very common distractor, but there are strategies to help you let go of these thoughts. This mindfulness technique will help you make a conscious choice about what you want to focus on by teaching you how to let ruminating thoughts just float away.

Practice this exercise in a quiet space with limited distractions. Sit comfortably and close your eyes. Take a moment to ground yourself by taking three deep breaths, inhaling and exhaling fully. Visualize yourself sitting peacefully on the edge of a gentle river or stream. Imagine beautiful fall leaves floating down this stream.

As you visualize this, ruminating thoughts will arise and try to distract you. Instead of resisting the thoughts, visualize taking each thought and placing it on a leaf in the stream. Then watch the thought as it calmly floats down the stream on the leaf. Eventually see the leaf far in the distance until it is out of your sight. Then gently refocus your attention on the gentle river. As thoughts continue to arise, keep envisioning placing them on a beautiful leaf and letting them float away.

This visualization is a great technique that will let you practice letting go of thoughts so you can concentrate on the present. Throughout your day, you can even use this metaphor to let go of distracting thoughts. The more you practice this mindfulness visualization, the greater your ability will be to let go of distracting thoughts and refocus on what matters to you in the moment.

RESOURCES

Guided Meditations

- **Focus Meditation album** by Dr. Tiffany Shelton Mariolle available at www.tiffanyshelton.com

- **Guided meditations** for concentration available on the Insight Timer app, available at https://insighttimer.com

Websites and Apps

- **BrainFM,** functional music to improve focus, www.brain.fm

- **Focus Me,** website and app blocker, https://focusme.com

- **Mindful Browsing,** gentle reminders when you visit time-wasting sites, www.mindfulbrowsing.org

- **PomoDoneApp,** Pomodoro Method app, https://pomodoneapp.com

Books

- *Focus: The Hidden Driver of Excellence,* by Daniel Goleman

- *The Happiness Trap: How to Stop Struggling and Start Living: A Guide to ACT,* by Dr. Russ Harris

- *Hardwiring Happiness: The New Brain Science of Contentment, Calm, and Confidence,* by Rick Hanson, PhD

- *The ONE Thing: The Surprisingly Simple Truth Behind Extraordinary Results,* by Gary Keller and Jay Papasan

REFERENCES

- Amen, Daniel. "7 Ways to Increase Dopamine, Focus, and Energy." *BrainMD*. Accessed June 19, 2019. Retrieved from www.brainmdhealth.com /blog/7-ways-to-boost-dopamine-focus-and -energy.

- Andrade, Jackie. "What Does Doodling Do?" *Applied Cognitive Psychology 24* (2009): 100–106. doi:10.1002/acp.1561.

- Dzulkifli, Mariam, and Muhammad Mustafar. "The Influence of Colour on Memory Performance: A Review." *The Malaysian Journal of Medical Sciences* 20 (2) (2013): 3–9. www.ncbi.nlm.nih.gov /pmc/articles/PMC3743993

- Julson, Erica. "10 Best Ways to Increase Dopamine Levels Naturally." Accessed May 10, 2018. www.healthline.com/nutrition/how-to-increase -dopamine.

- Simon, Harvey. "Giving Thanks Can Make You Happier." Harvard Health Publishing. www.health.harvard.edu/healthbeat /giving-thanks-can-make-you-happier.

INDEX

ABOUT THE AUTHOR

Dr. Tiffany Shelton Mariolle is a psychologist, author, and entrepreneur helping people find peace within their minds, brains, and spirits. She combines her expertise in psychology, neuropsychology, meditation, and entrepreneurship to help people cope with life's stressors and go from feeling overwhelmed by life to thriving in it. Whether it's with her readers, patients, or Conscious Life Shop customers, her mission is to help folks take care of their mental, brain, and spiritual health.

Dr. Mariolle fulfills her purpose to help folks find peace with meditation albums, writings, online content, teaching, research, and psychological services. Find out more about Dr. Tiffany Shelton Mariolle on her website, www.tiffanyshelton.com.

CPSIA information can be obtained
at www.ICGtesting.com
Printed in the USA
LVHW010314040320
648922LV00003B/4